To Dad

Happy Easter

"78"

Bill

This Was New England

Books by Martin W. Sandler

The People Make a Nation

The Restless Americans
[with Edwin C. Rozwenc and Edward C. Martin]

In Search of America

This Was Connecticut

This Was New England

New Hampshire coast, c. 1890   Photographer unknown

This Was New England

Images of a Vanished Past

Martin W. Sandler

New York Graphic Society   Boston

First Edition

T 10/77

Lines from "Lilacs" are reprinted from *The Complete Poetical Works of Amy Lowell,* published by Houghton Mifflin Company in 1955.

LIBRARY OF CONGRESS CATALOGING IN PUBLICATION DATA

Sandler, Martin W.
    This was New England.

    1. New England—Description and travel—Views.
I. Title.
F5.S23   917.4'04'40222   77-8604
ISBN 0-8212-0715-6

New York Graphic Society Books are published by Little, Brown and Company

Published simultaneously in Canada by Little, Brown & Company (Canada) Limited
Printed in the United States of America

For two remarkable people —
Edward and Sylvia Weiss —
with love and appreciation

*. . . here was the passionate enigma of New England felt:
New England, with its harsh and stony soil, and its tragic and
lonely beauty; its desolate rocky coasts and its swarming
fisheries, the white, piled, frozen bleakness of its winters with
the magnificent jewelry of stars, the dark firwoods, and the
warm little white houses at which it is impossible to look without thinking of groaning bins, hung bacon, hard cider, succu-
lent bastings . . . And then . . . the coming of spring and
ecstasy, and overnight the thrum of wings, the burst of the
tender buds, the ripple and dance of the roughened water, the
light of flowers, the sudden, fleeting, almost captured, and
exultant spring.*

—THOMAS WOLFE, Of Time and the River

Milford, Connecticut, 1908

W. H. Horton

Contents

Gardiner, Maine, 1914   Bertrand H. Wentworth

Introduction

*Behind every book is the story of how the book came to be.
This Was New England* is no exception. Between the
years 1970 and 1975 I wrote three American history
texts. Much of the material in my textbooks is based on
visual evidence — photographs, paintings, cartoons,
advertisements — of the eras being treated. The
rationale for this approach is the fact that in dealing with
today's students we are dealing with perhaps the most
visually oriented generation of youngsters since the in-
vention of movable type. What has fascinated me especially is the reception that these books have received
from adults. Regularly the mail brings such comments
as "If only we had been taught history this way" or "It *is*
true, a picture *is* worth a thousand words." Often the
correspondents refer to a particular photograph show-
ing people engaged in a long-lost activity or to a series
of photographs that conveys the character of a particular
neighborhood or region; for in the past decade there has
been a tremendous increase in the appreciation of
photographs as social documents. It would not be reach-
ing too far to state that we are at a point where
documentary photography is coming to be regarded as a
true art form.

When I set out on my quest for the New England past
my methods and my interest were not new to me. First
of all, my search for materials for my textbooks had led
me to scores of collections of negatives and prints. Second, my interest in New England is inbred. I was born
in New England, raised in New England, have played,
worked, taught, and vacationed in practically every area
of this region. Most important, I feel that I am truly a
representative New Englander. For better or worse,

there is no *Mayflower* or even *Speedwell* in my background. We are a nation of immigrants; I am a New England representative of the melting pot — or salad bowl, if you will.

Yet with all this background I was totally unprepared for what lay ahead of me in my quest. Even with my previous forays into pictorial archives, I had no idea of the monumental number of photographs I would encounter. Much of the research for my history texts was carried on in the great (and still largely untapped) photographic troves of this nation's capital. I had known that there were marvelous collections of early New England photographs in such places as the Library of Congress and the National Archives. But I had made the decision to stay out of Washington until I "exhausted" whatever New England sources I could find. Exhausted! My chief problem has been to find a place for even some of the magnificent Library of Congress photographs I discovered.

In fact, what has happened is that I have discovered enough significant photographs to fill ten books; I have begun a large New England glass plate negative collection of my own; and Louie Howland, my editor, friend, and fellow enthusiast, has been pleading with me for months to consider this particular book finished.

This Was New England contains 240 photographs. As I look through the log that I kept as I did my research, I find that I examined more than 500,000 glass plate negatives in order to select the 6,000 "finalists" from which these 240 photographs were chosen. The odometer in my car tells me that I traveled more than 35,000 miles up and down and across New England to obtain the visual record contained in the pages that follow. The search has been challenging and exhausting. It has also been a pure delight. It has been so not only because of the

photographs that I found but, just as important, because of the ways in which they were found and the people I have encountered throughout my search.

For example, I remember the first time I went to the New Hampshire Historical Society. I had had a telephone conversation with curator Rick Franz the week before and when I met him at the society my first question was, "How big a staff do you have?" "My staff is five foot, nine and you're looking at him," Franz said. What I came to find out in the months that followed was that Rick Franz's situation was typical of most historical societies. Dedicated, intelligent, enthusiastic people were struggling to preserve the record of the past without adequate funds, staff, or facilities. People like Phillip Purrington at the New Bedford Whaling Museum, Marsha Peters at the Rhode Island Historical Society, and Dan Lohnes at the Society for the Preservation of New England Antiquities were working against tremendous financial odds to conserve these vital records before they literally faded away.

This is particularly true of the chief source of early photographs, glass plate negatives, which are the "stepchildren" among all the various holdings of the historical societies. In most societies these negatives are piled by the thousands in wooden or cardboard boxes in basement or attic. Unless proper preservative measures are taken, they will eventually self-destruct. Yet more than any other type of historical material, they provide us with an actual view of the way people looked, dressed, worked, and played. They give us a striking record of landmarks long since vanished and values, occupations, and life-styles that are gone forever.

To return to Rick Franz and the New Hampshire Historical Society. Not only did Franz lead me to a vast collection of negatives of New Hampshire life from the

1850s through the early 1900s but he then took me to the top floor of the society building. There, on that steamy June day, I was to experience the first of what came to be many adventures in the art of early New England photograph collecting. Once we had made the hike to the top floor, Rick pointed to a long series of large volumes on the top row of the bookshelves, some twenty feet in the air. "Up there," he said, "are the sixty-six George Dewey Abbot scrapbooks. There are a lot of good early photographs in them but they're kind of hard to get at."

Hard to get at! The only way to get to them was up the library ladder which was fastened flush against the bookshelves. The books were large, bulky, and jammed one against the other. Twenty feet in the air, with one hand clutched frantically onto the rung of the ladder, there was no way I could even peek inside a volume. So sixty-six times up the ladder and sixty-six times down I went with several missteps and near catastrophes in between. But the exercise was worth the effort; these volumes contained some of the finest pictures of life in early New Hampshire I was to find.

How decorous is the life of the author! On my hands and knees in the basement of the Society for the Preservation of New England Antiquities, where I pored through glass negatives of life in the early Massachusetts communities of Essex and Greenwich, now permanently buried under the Quabbin Reservoir. Carrying heavy wooden boxes from the loft of an ancient barn near Stowe, Vermont. (How excited I was to have discovered the magnificent views of early farm life in what the owner believed to be Maine and Vermont. What frustration in finding on closer inspection that the signs on the barns and village stores were all in French and that the photographs taken by an early itinerant New England photographer were of farm areas in nineteenth-century Quebec.)

Yet as is the case with all worthwhile endeavors I came to accept the fact that the frustrations go hand in glove with the successes. I was ecstatic to find a selection of more than 350 magnificent photographs taken by the Cape Cod maritime photographer H. K. Cummings: pictures of the saltworks that once dominated the Buzzards Bay shoreline; pictures of the first digging of the Cape Cod Canal; awesome scenes of ships and men run aground. Yet as I savored my good fortune I was told it was too bad that I hadn't gotten at the other 5,000 Cummings negatives before they peeled the emulsion away and used the glass to make greenhouses.

But overall my search involved many more successes than failures. High on the list of these successes was my fortuitous meeting with a lovely woman, Mrs. Edith LaFrancis, and the chance to study her collection of photographs by the brothers George and Alvah Howes. In two previously published books I had seen two fine pictures of life in nineteenth-century western Massachusetts. Each of these pictures carried the credit line: "Collection of Mrs. Edith LaFrancis." The photographs were so striking that I was determined to find Mrs. La-Francis and go through her collection. I called the publishers of each of the two books and was told that Mrs. LaFrancis had been an elderly woman at the time of their publication and that she was probably "now deceased."

How could one who had faced death at the New Hampshire Historical Society accept such a pronouncement without question? I proceeded to check with the information operators in every town in western Massachusetts. Time and again I was told that there was no listing for a Mrs. Edith LaFrancis. So I began calling at random people named LaFrancis in each of the major western Massachusetts communities. Perhaps I could find a relative. On my third call to Agawam I struck gold. "Yes," the lady said, "I know of Edith LaFrancis; I happen to be her."

What has followed has been the growth of a valued friendship in which Edith LaFrancis and I have spent hours studying the Howes brothers negatives in her collection, cataloguing them, identifying them wherever possible, and absorbing the genius of these two itinerant nineteenth-century photographers who captured the spirit and character of the people and the age in which they lived.

The Howes brothers were wonderful photographers. Their work would have been outstanding in any era. One of the unexpected joys in my quest for pictures of the New England past was my discovery not only of single great photographs but of a growing ability to find and identify the products of individual New England photographers. For example, just as a lover of American paintings comes to attention when unexpectedly encountering a Homer or a Mount or a Bingham that he or she has never seen before, so have I found myself exclaiming, "Good grief, that's a Baldwin Coolidge" or "I'll bet my soul that's a Stebbins." And these encounters occur in the unlikeliest places. Two weeks before I succumbed to my editor's deadline I found twenty-five Howes brothers negatives in a flea market in Saco, Maine. After agonizing over which of the Baldwin Coolidge photographs I should use from the Society for the Preservation of New England Antiquities I found what "had to be" Coolidge photographs in Nantucket, in the Vermont Historical Society, and in Biddeford Pool, Maine. How proud I was when, in each instance, the photographs did prove to be the work of Mr. Coolidge.

Unfortunately, the photographers of many of the pictures in this book will never be known. The photographs have been chosen for content and aesthetic quality and often the negatives from which they were taken were unlabeled as to the photographer. But there remains the majority to whom proper credit can be given.

Deep in the bowels of the Library of Congress I encountered the work of the nineteenth-century New England photographer Charles H. Currier. His work is among the most striking I have seen. Since that first encounter, I have become friendly with Ernst Halbestadt of Onset, Massachusetts. It was he who donated the Currier images to the Library of Congress after rescuing them by purchasing the negatives for six dollars from a woman who was about to sell them off to be used as window glass. One of my wife's friends told me of a woman in Lee, New Hampshire, who had some glass negatives. My trip to Lee resulted in a beautiful day spent visiting with Mrs. Jean Nugent. Midway through our conversation Jean brought out a large cardboard box. "I bought these in an old barn sale," she said. "You might find them interesting. They were taken by a photographer named Ulric Bourgeois." Interesting! The negatives Jean Nugent proceeded to show me included a series of sixty-five pictures that Mr. Bourgeois had taken of a nineteenth-century Manchester, New Hampshire, hermit named C. L. Lambert. Space has permitted the use of only a few of these photographs but in my opinion they are among the most important in the whole book.

As was the case in so many instances, once I "discovered" another photographer, I then stumbled upon an important or delightful anecdote about some aspect of his or her work. For example, I later found out that Ulric Bourgeois was one of the first photographers to blow his images up to large sizes. In 1900, a store in downtown Manchester, New Hampshire, hung some of these images in their windows. One of the pictures showed couples on a beach. A local resident walked down the street, looked at the picture, saw her husband on the blanket with another woman, and subpoenaed the photograph. It was, I am sure, one of the first times in American history that a photograph was used as the basis for a divorce proceeding!

My foraging up and down across Cape Cod led me not only to many important individual pictures but to the works of such early photographers as Edward Sprague, Frederic Perry, and H. K. Cummings. In Vermont, I spent three days sitting on a front porch in Williamsville, as Mrs. Porter Thayer lovingly brought me out box after box of glass negatives that her husband had taken at the turn of the century. "Some of the best pictures," she told me, "were of individuals and groups but when he retired Porter took them to the dump and destroyed them. He didn't want anyone to make money in years to come off of people who wouldn't be around to share in the benefits." How frustrating. How understandable.

Some of the collections I examined turned out to be so vast and exciting that they stunned me. I remember my first call to Rob Egleston at the New Haven Colony Historical Society during which Rob informed me that, yes, they had lots of old glass plate negatives, but had been so busy with other top-priority projects since he had come on the job that he wasn't sure just what was in the collection. Off to New Haven I went. This was to be one of the most significant of my trips, for there in New Haven I discovered a collection so superior in content and quality that it was obvious at once that it warranted a book of its own. Most of the more than 45,000 nega-

tives in the New Haven collection were taken by a photographer named T. S. Bronson. By the time I had completed my third two-day trip to the society, I had reached an agreement with executive director J. J. Smith, Rob Egleston, and assistant curator Dave Corrigan that we should indeed do an entire book on the New Haven collection. My publisher was equally struck by the beauty and content of the Bronson photographs and *This Was Connecticut* was born.

There were several trips to the Rhode Island Historical Society, where curator Marsha Peters shared with me both her enthusiasm over the large holdings in the society and her excitement over the fact that someone finally wanted to research the collection and use the pictures.

Finally, there were all the local libraries, museums, auctions, flea markets, college collections, and private holdings too numerous to mention where I either found a picture that has made its way into this book or was inspired with an idea of a kind of picture that would have to be included in a book about a New England long since vanished. Mention must also be made of the dozens of individuals who spent hours speaking with me about the New England past and who either led me to specific collections or supplied me with vital information and anecdotes so important to this book. I hope that I have paid proper credit to each of them in this book's acknowledgment page.

Here, then, is basically how I came to find the pictures from which the final selections were made. But what were the bases for my selections and how was an organizational format decided upon? As I mentioned earlier I looked at more than 500,000 pictures in compiling *This Was New England*. Obviously the final selection process was as difficult as the picture-finding itself. Ultimately I decided upon three criteria for picture selection: first, the aesthetic quality of the picture itself and the human quality portrayed in the photograph; second, the type of activity portrayed in the photograph, with special consideration given to scenes of activities long since vanished; and third, the manner in which each photograph conveys the character of the people who made New England.

But in the end it was, of course, New England itself that dictated what was to go and what was to stay. If the book was to live up to its title and its intent then the ultimate criterion had to be: how well did each picture convey an enduring visual memory of New England?

The same is true as far as the organization of the book is concerned, for, in truth, the nature of New England itself thrust the organization upon me. New England is a diverse, varied region, made up of mountains, rolling hills, river valleys, hard coast, soft coast, remote areas, teeming cities — and always the sea. Activities native to one area are not always native to another. So it is the terrain which defines the people and their activities — not mere political boundaries. A fisherman in Maine, for example, has always had much more in common with a fisherman in Rhode Island than with an industrialist in his own state.

The people in these photographs were New Englanders. That is obvious from the locale of each picture. But as one who has studied early photographs from all over this nation, I cannot help but be struck with the universality of this collection. Were the people happier than we are today? Were they healthier or wiser? Who is to say? What is obvious is that there was a time when things were different and people led different lives. It is important that we recognize these differences, for they have much to tell us about the durability of our heritage in the present day.

Finally, some special acknowledgments are in order: to John Wilmerding, whose encouragement and enthusiasm is so appreciated and whose plea to select quality over all other criteria has been, I hope, well taken; to Louie Howland, who shared the joys of discovery, the agonies of selection, whose advice was always on target, and who dealt with the task of keeping a perpetually ecstatic author on an even keel; to Chuck Spooner, who is a genuine genius in the art of developing glass plate negatives; and to my wife, Carol, who kept me and the entire project organized, who shared so much of the travel, and who became not only a co-enthusiast but a co-worker as well.

This Was New England

Wallingford, Connecticut, c. 1910   T. S. Bronson

On the Move

South Newfane, Vermont, 1905   Porter Thayer

OLD ELM TREE. SO. NEWFANE. VT.

I find the great thing in this world is not so much where we stand, as in what direction we are moving.

To reach the port of heaven, we must sail sometimes with the wind and sometimes against it — but we must sail, and not drift, nor lie at anchor.

— OLIVER WENDELL HOLMES
The Autocrat of the Breakfast Table

Manchester, New Hampshire, c. 1900
Ulric Bourgeois

The nineteenth century began with New Englanders, like all Americans, dependent upon the horse, the wind, and shanks' mare for travel. It ended with man on the verge of sailing through the air. Nothing until the advent of nuclear power changed our way of life more dramatically than did the steam engine. There are those who would question whether it was a change for the better.

As the transportation revolution gathered momentum, photographers were on hand to record its effects. Yet they were clearly torn between their desire to record what was novel and what was traditional. Scenes such as those on pages 18, 20, and 22 reveal that, if the pace was much slower then, travelers at least had ample time to appreciate the view.

The increasing mobility of Yankees, who could travel by train, steamboat (both side-wheel and "propellor"), trolley, and finally internal combustion automobile, radically reshaped New England, socially as well as economically. It tied farmers and country people ever closer to the cities. It facilitated the spread of suburbs (and gave rise to a whole new class of workers — the commuters). It was part and parcel of the Industrial Age.

A mixed blessing? Of course. But few of us would turn down the opportunity to sail to New York City on one of the great Fall River Line steamers or to take our ease in the parlor car of a crack passenger train, secure (more or less) in the knowledge that we would reach our appointed destination on time and in one piece.

New Hampshire, c. 1885   Photographer unknown

At the top, Mt. Washington, New Hampshire, c. 1880   Photographer unknown

Derby, Connecticut, 1902

T. S. Bronson

The Gay Head taxi, Gay Head, Massachusetts, c. 1885

Albert Cook Church

Williamsville, Vermont, 1902

Porter Thayer

Providence, Rhode Island, 1886
Photographer unknown

World's biggest tricycle,
Concord, New Hampshire, c. 1900
Photographer unknown

Greenfield, Massachusetts, 1890   Photographer unknown

New Bedford, Massachusetts, c. 1890   Photographer unknown

Mt. Washington, New Hampshire, 1889
Photographer unknown

Enfield, Massachusetts, c. 1900
Photographer unknown

Lake Winnepesaukee, New Hampshire, 1916   Photographer unknown

Lake Winnepesaukee, New Hampshire, 1916
Photographer unknown

Waterbury, Vermont, c. 1915
Photographer unknown

Bethel, Connecticut, 1905

T. S. Bronson

Portsmouth, New Hampshire, 1905

Photographer unknown

Funeral sleigh(?), Burlington, Vermont, 1878
Photographer unknown

Mansfield Grove, Connecticut, 1906
T. S. Bronson

Camden, Maine, 1904

Photographer unknown

The Sea

At the wheel, c. 1915   Photographer unknown

There you stand, a hundred feet above the silent decks, striding along the deep, as if the masts were gigantic stilts, while beneath you and between your legs, as if it were, swim the hugest monsters of the sea. . . . There you stand, lost in the infinite series of the sea, with nothing ruffled but the waves.

—HERMAN MELVILLE, Moby Dick

Fishing vessel Columbia, *c. 1923*
Albert Cook Church

Whaling crew, 1881
Marian Smith

In the beginning, the sea provided the lifeline between colonies and mother country. But it was also the sea that gave New Englanders a seemingly endless supply of food and a wide variety of occupations connected with shipping, fishing, and commerce.

New England vessels traded in ports around the world. Vessels from a dozen New England towns cruised the world's whaling grounds in search of the monsters of the deep. This marriage with the sea not only resulted in generations of New England sailors, riggers, coopers, shipwrights, fishermen, and the like, but also produced the great number of coastal ports and towns which continue to attract the photographer, the painter, and the vacationist.

Nothing brings back these seafaring days more vividly than do the photographs of such nineteenth and early twentieth century photographers as N. L. Stebbins (page 57), H. K. Cummings (page 56), and Albert Cook Church (pages 40, 46, and 47), who dealt almost exclusively with maritime subjects.

There were countless other New England photographers who, while not concentrating on any one subject, captured the lure and flavor of the sea. An unknown New England photographer (page 53), for example, captured the beautiful image of one of the many saltworks along the southern New England coast.

And finally, there were those who went to sea themselves and took their camera along. One such photographer was Mrs. Marian Smith, who accompanied her husband, the master of a whaling vessel, on his long voyages around the world. Her photographs (page 40) give us a nonromanticized view of this harsh and taxing life. Another of these seafaring photographers was Charles E. Bolles, whose photographs include the dramatic view of the *Governor Ames,* said to be the first five-masted schooner ever built (page 45).

U.S.S. Constitution, *Portsmouth, New Hampshire, 1858*   Photographer unknown

Portland, Maine, c. 1890   Photographer unknown

Launching of the James E. Newsome,
Booth Bay Harbor, Maine, 1919
Photographer unknown

Portland, Maine, c. 1900
Photographer unknown

Waldoboro, Maine, c. 1895   Charles E. Bolles

Cuttyhunk, Massachusetts

Albert Cook Church

Top mast man   Albert Cook Church

Wreck of the Empress, *Kennebunkport, Maine, 1894*
A. B. Houdlette

Gloucester, Massachusetts, 1890

Charles H. Currier

Convict ship, Portland, Maine, c. 1900
Photographer unknown

Barnstable, Massachusetts, 1891
Frederic Perry

Drying the cod, Gloucester, Massachusetts, c. 1900
Photographer unknown

Saltworks, Padanaram, Massachusetts, c. 1880   Photographer unknown

Cape Cod, Massachusetts, c. 1880

Frederic Perry

Gardiner, Maine, 1914   Bertrand H. Wentworth

Orleans, Massachusetts, c. 1895
H. K. Cummings

Regatta, Boston Harbor, c. 1890

N. L. Stebbins

Isle of Shoals, New Hampshire, 1902
Henry Peabody

Biddeford Pool, Maine, 1907

Baldwin Coolidge

The Farm

Vermont, c. 1880   Photographer unknown

Early and late the farmer has gone forth with his formidable scythe, weapons of time, Time's weapon, and fought the ground inch by inch. It is the summer's enterprise. And if we were a more poetic people, horns would be blown to celebrate its completion. There might be a Haymaker's Day. New England's peaceful battles. At Bunker Hill there were some who stood at the rail fence and behind the winrows of new-mown hay. They have not yet quitted the field. They stand there still; they alone have not retreated.

—HENRY DAVID THOREAU
Journal, II, 393–395, August 17, 1851

New Hampshire, c. 1880
John S. Wright

Kingston, Rhode Island, 1891
Photographer unknown

Living off the land has always been difficult in New England. The growing season is short and the soil is as notable for its rocks as for its produce. The first settlers had no choice but to work the land, and throughout the nineteenth century farming was an essential part of New England life. Today, in an era when more than seventy percent of all Americans live in cities, many of us can still trace our beginnings to such scenes as that on page 64.

Some fine early New England photographers were themselves farmers. Porter Thayer, for example, was well versed in the art of maple-sugaring and his photographs of this classic New England enterprise (pages 66 and 67) show an understanding of the process that is palpable. Others, if not active farmers, displayed a genuine respect for farming. Baldwin Coolidge (page 60), John S. Wright (page 79), and Charles H. Currier (page 64) were obviously anxious to capture the essential dignity of New England farm life. Others, like the Howes brothers, left us with a vivid chronicle of particular aspects of farming — such as tobacco-raising in the Connecticut Valley (pages 72 to 75).

One photographer (page 76), like New England's fabled weather, presented us with the unpredictable. And finally, another unknown photographer, either through design or by magnificent accident, gave us a New England farm photograph so remarkable (page 61) that one has to look at it more than once before becoming convinced that it is indeed a photograph and not a painting.

Country kitchen, Maine, 1901

Charles H. Currier

Bedford, New Hampshire, c. 1895
Ulric Bourgeois

Wethersfield, Connecticut, c. 1895
Howes Brothers

Dover, Vermont, c. 1905

Porter Thayer

Dover, Vermont, c. 1905   Porter Thayer

Newfane, Vermont, c. 1900
Porter Thayer

BELOW:
LEFT, Western Massachusetts, c. 1890
Howes Brothers

RIGHT, Agawam, Massachusetts, c. 1895
Howes Brothers

Burlington, Vermont, c. 1895   Photographer unknown

East Haven, Connecticut, 1908
T. S. Bronson

Western Massachusetts, c. 1895
Howes Brothers

Suffield, Connecticut, c. 1895
Howes Brothers

Suffield, Connecticut, c. 1895

Howes Brothers

Suffield, Connecticut, c. 1895
Howes Brothers

Suffield, Connecticut, c. 1895
Howes Brothers

Suffield, Connecticut, c. 1895

Howes Brothers

Vermont, c. 1870
Photographer unknown

Kingston, Rhode Island, 1891   Photographer unknown

Deerfield, Massachusetts, c. 1895
Howes Brothers

New Hampshire, c. 1880

John S. Wright

Boston, Massachusetts, c. 1890

Photographer unknown

People

Jail keeper, York, Maine, 1878   Photographer unknown

. . . *because I am New England,*
Because my roots are in it,
Because my leaves are of it,
Because my flowers are for it,
Because it is my country
And I speak to it of itself
And sing of it with my own voice
Since certainly it is mine.

—AMY LOWELL, *"Lilacs"*

Ludlow, Vermont, c. 1915
Photographer unknown

In poring over the hundreds of photographs from which I selected "finalists" for this section, I was continually reminded of two New England quotations that have long been favorites. The first was written by the poet Anne Bradstreet in the seventeenth century:

If we had no winter, the spring would not be pleasant
If we did not sometimes taste of adversity, prosperity
would not be so welcome

The second was written by the consummate nineteenth-century Yankee, Dr. Oliver Wendell Holmes:

For the Puritan still lives in New England, thank God! and will live there so long as New England lives and keeps her old renown. New England is not dead yet. She still is mother of a race of conquerors, — stern men, little given to the expression of their feelings, sometimes careless of the graces, but fertile, tenacious, and knowing only duty. Each of you, as I do, thinks of a hundred such that he has known.

Nineteenth-century New Englanders seem to have been particularly affected by their topography, climate, and way of life. This is revealed in photograph after photograph. Consider the family portrait by Charles H. Currier (page 88). The patriarch is ever present, even in death. The dour Maine jail keeper (page 81) is another image full of portent. But perhaps most revealing of all is the photograph on page 82. In itself, it is a striking image of nineteenth-century New Englanders. It takes on an added dimension when we learn that the unpretentious gentleman posed behind his mother is John Garabaldi Sargent, who later became attorney general of the United States under Calvin Coolidge.

Orleans, Massachusetts, c. 1885   H. K. Cummings

New Haven, Connecticut, c. 1890   Myron T. Filley

Dover, Vermont, 1898
Porter Thayer

Littleton, New Hampshire, 1889
W. Kilburn

Women's Christian Temperance Union,
Newfane, Vermont, c. 1910
Porter Thayer

Life Saving Crew, Hull, Massachusetts, 1893
Baldwin Coolidge

Visitors' Day, Massachusetts State Guard, 1890
Charles H. Currier

Mt. Desert Island, Maine, 1895
Charles H. Currier

Boston, Massachusetts, 1895

Charles H. Currier

Western Massachusetts, c. 1895

Howes Brothers

Haying time, Mattapan, Massachusetts, c. 1880

Henry L. Hadcock

Sconsett (Nantucket), Massachusetts, c. 1900
Baldwin Coolidge

Brattleboro, Vermont, 1902
Porter Thayer

Students, Brown University,
Providence, Rhode Island, c. 1890
Photographer unknown

NAVAL TRAINING STATION Newport
SWIMMING INSTRUCTION

Swimming instruction, Naval Training Station, Newport, Rhode Island, 1891   Photographer unknown

Boston, Massachusetts, 1893
Charles H. Currier

Barnstable, Massachusetts, c. 1900
Frederic Perry

New Bedford, Massachusetts, 1889   Photographer unknown

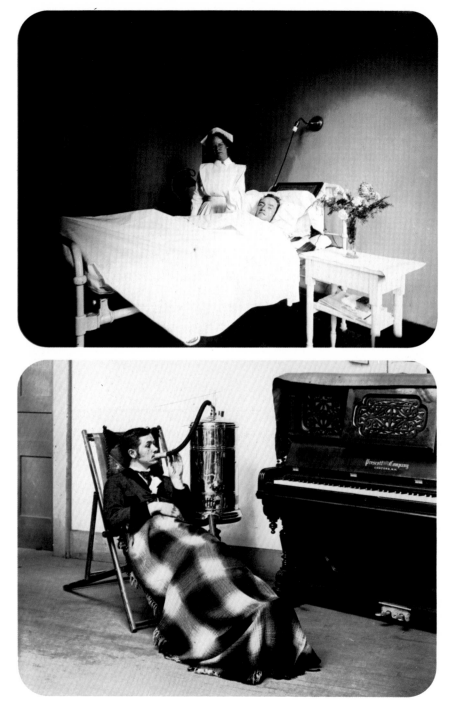

New Haven, Connecticut, c. 1905
T. S. Bronson

Concord, New Hampshire, c. 1890
Photographer unknown

Civil War veteran, Buzzards Bay, Massachusetts, 1894   Photographer unknown

Maine, 1895

Charles H. Currier

Rhode Island, c. 1885   John S. Wright

The Hermit of Manchester

From the Manchester (New Hampshire) *Mirror,* September, 1901

Among the many interesting things to be found in Manchester there is perhaps none more interesting than and certainly more unique than the Mosquito Pond hermit, Charles Lambert. Both he and his dwelling are objects of curiosity to many and his place is visited by hundreds of people during the summer season. . . . His crops are mainly herbs which he sells to local druggists and for years this business has been the leading source from which his revenue has been derived. . . . On the *Mirror* man making himself known, together with his occupation, the old gentleman was for a time rather averse to conversation, but soon was led to talk and display some of his treasures. First the museum of Indian relics and minerals was examined and some of the Indian arrow heads are very fine indeed. A flint hammer head and gouges in a good state of preservation, together with some pieces of stone cooking utensils, are also embraced in the collection. Mr. Lambert takes great pride in everything in his museum, and with him to explain each and every article in his own inimitable style is well worth the trip to his place from the city. . . .

The old Mill dam, the ruins of which still remain, furnished the power to run the first sawmill in Manchester. It was one of the earliest erected in the state. Here ran the road from Concord to Boston, and in this vicinity was erected the first blacksmith shop to be found for miles around. Passing from one spot to another with Mr. Lambert, the *Mirror* man was treated to such a dose of local history regarding every stick and stone on the place that he had very little opportunity to question Mr. Lambert about himself. He glories in his place and manner of living, and with his cats and sheep is as happy as he wants to be. For over forty years he has been accumulating considerable property. When he first settled on the banks of the Cohas he bought about forty acres and today owns a tract of country that stretches along the banks of the Cohas a full mile. In his early days here he farmed his land and had in his charge many sheep beside his own for which he received a certain sum for shearing and care. At that time there were 1200 sheep kept in the Mosquito Pond district where today there is probably not one hundred.

Mr. Lambert gained his knowledge of sheep husbandry in England, as he was born in Lincolnshire, on the downs famous the world over as home of the famous South Down sheep.

There in a little hut made of stone from the seashore, cemented with mortar and covered with a thatch of straw, Charles Lambert first saw the light of day, sixty-three years ago. In early life he showed a disposition to inquire into the mysteries of plant life, and following this inclination as he grew older he found employment gathering herbs for apothecaries and chemists engaged in the manufacture of medicines. Possessing but the mere rudiments of an education, he, as he grew older in following this occupation studied with avidity works on botany and the properties of the plants he sought, as well as delving deeply in the grand old book of nature, soon had at his command a profound knowledge of botanical science, which today is his pride and joy. In this occupation Mr. Lambert travelled much in Great Britain, France, and other European countries until he reached his majority, when he decided to come to America, arriving in New York just after the accession of Filmore to the presidency of the United States. Travelling throughout New York, New Jersey, Pennsylvania, and Massachusetts, he at last reached New Hampshire, where he settled in in the Mosquito Pond district and has since made his home. Mr. Lambert is of medium size, considerably grey, but carries in his head a pair of bright brown eyes that in his younger days might have proved attractive to the opposite sex. But from the lonely life he has led and his evident aversion to the company of the opposite sex, the world at large is imbued with the idea that he was unfortunate in some attachment formed when he was young and decided that once out would be all one for him. Mr. Lambert, when in the mood, entertains his visitors with songs and recitations of poetry of his own composition, and is a quiet inoffensive old man. His tastes are simple and his wants are few. He does not use tobaccos or liquors at all and until his sickness of the past summer had never tasted either tea or coffee as a beverage. . . .

Mr. Lambert has never forsworn his allegiance to the English government and is still a loyal subject of her majesty. He is rather Democratic in his ideas and is not an ardent advocate of a protective tariff system. He reads the papers of the day and keeps posted on what is going on in the world, and at parting with the *Mirror* man, invited him to come again, and stated that he intended to come to Manchester about Christmas time and bring up his museum and place it on exhibition. Should he do that, one thing is certain. Charles Lambert will be one of the most interesting objects in the whole collection.

Manchester, New Hampshire, c. 1895   Ulric Bourgeois

Manchester, New Hampshire, c. 1895
Ulric Bourgeois

Boston, Massachusetts, 1902

Baldwin Coolidge

The City

Evicted, c. 1900   Photographer unknown

New England haunted the minds of Americans, who tried to read its riddle, as if for their souls' good they must know what it meant. What was the truth about it? — and there were reasons for this obsession, for, generally speaking, Americans had a stake in New England. They were deeply implicated in it, as the seat of their deepest, their stoutest, their greatest tradition. Their blood was mixed perhaps with other strains, and perhaps they had long lived in other regions, but New England was their ark of the covenant still. How fared this ark? Into what hands had it fallen? . . . it meant much to Americans that this old region should fare well, as their palladium of truth, justice, freedom and learning. They could not rest until they were reconciled to it, and until it was reconciled to them.

—VAN WYCK BROOKS, Indian Summer

ABOVE: *Boston, Massachusetts, 1898*
   Henry Peabody

York Beach, Maine, 1905
Henry Peabody

In 1800 the United States was a nation of farms and villages. Less than three percent of our people lived in what could properly be called cities. But by 1900, given the inexorable pressures of the Industrial Revolution, more than thirty percent of all Americans were city people — and the figure was constantly rising.

New England cities tended to be larger in area, if not in density of population, than those in other parts of the country. This was so because many farms were included within city boundaries. (Although many Bostonians may not realize it, there are still working farms on the greater Boston tax rolls.)

Nineteenth-century New England cities displayed all the extremes of wealth and poverty, comfort and misery that are their portion today. All the opportunities for employment (page 114) and entertainment (page 115). All the hazards to health and safety. And all, or at least most, of the temptations — as well as opportunities for self-improvement of the mind and spirit.

One photograph seems particularly symbolic of city life a century ago. The black woman in the photograph on page 105 lived in New Bedford, Massachusetts. When her landlord refused to make badly needed repairs on the house she was renting, she withheld payment of the rent. The landlord then boarded up the windows and chimneys of the house and literally smoked her out. The photograph was taken moments after the woman and her children had fled the house.

Dexter, Maine, 1847
B. L. Ball

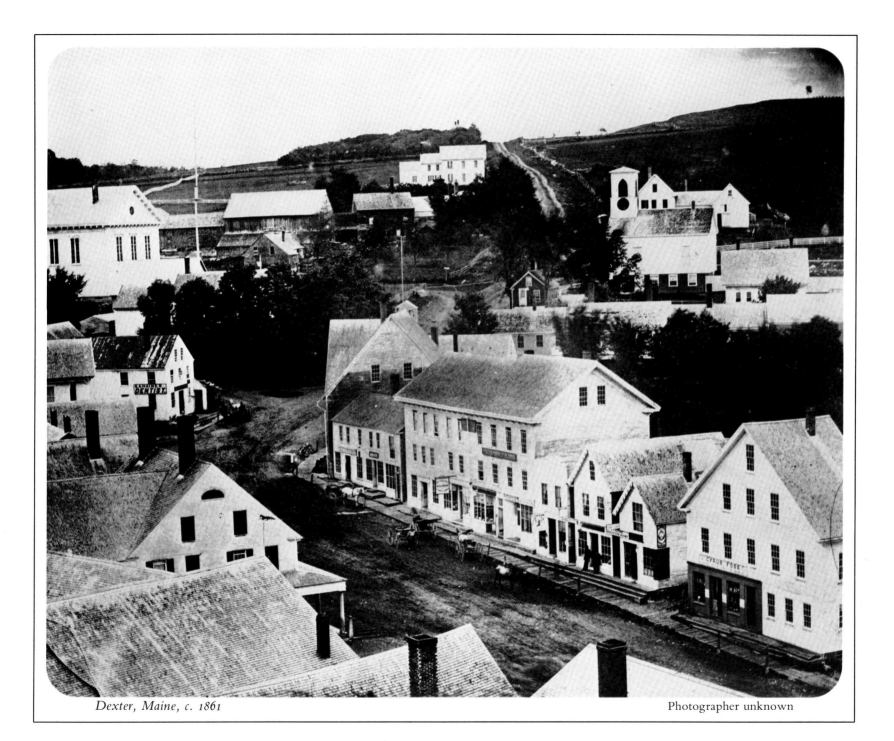

Dexter, Maine, c. 1861   Photographer unknown

Providence, Rhode Island, 1899

Photographer unknown

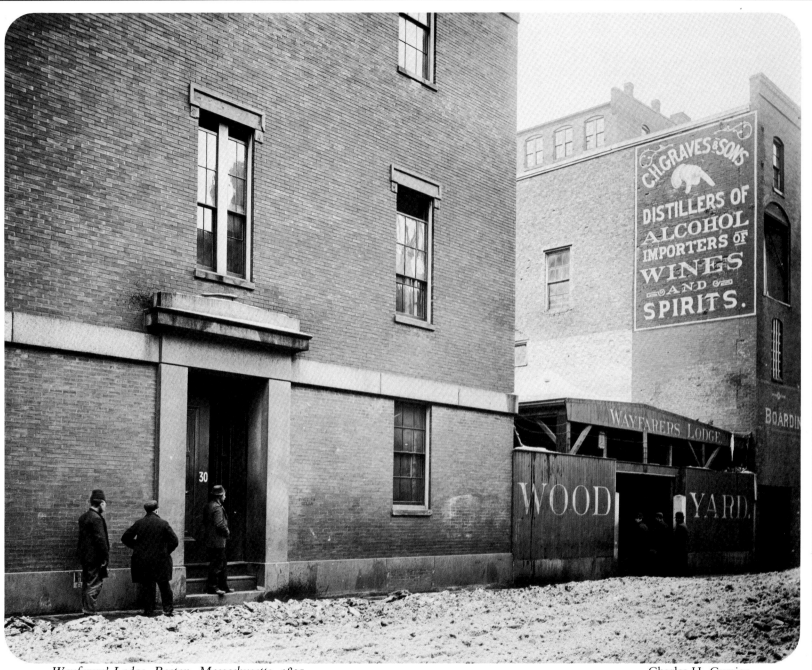

Wayfarers' Lodge, Boston, Massachusetts, 1895   Charles H. Currier

New Bedford, Massachusetts, c. 1880   Photographer unknown

Boston, Massachusetts, 1895

Charles H. Currier

New Haven, Connecticut, 1907

T. S. Bronson

Providence, Rhode Island, c. 1905   Photographer unknown

Human flag, Providence, Rhode Island, 1910

Photographer unknown

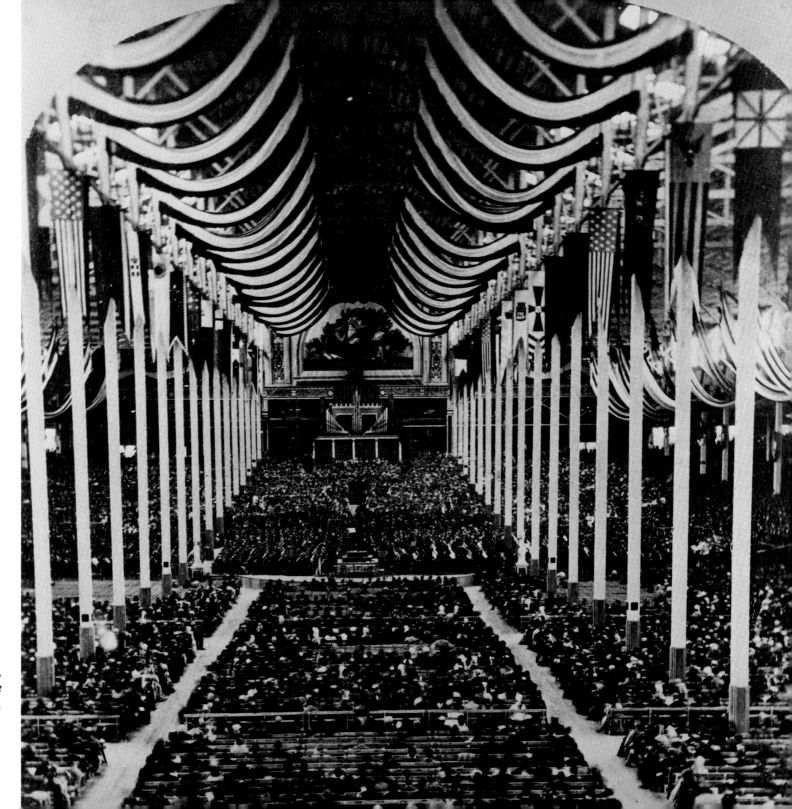

World Peace Jubilee,
Boston, Massachusetts, 1872
Photographer unknown

Northampton, Massachusetts, c. 1900   Photographer unknown

Boston, Massachusetts, 1902

Baldwin Coolidge

Northampton, Massachusetts, c. 1890
Photographer unknown

Photographers at fire, Boston, Massachusetts, c. 1890
Photographer unknown

Providence, Rhode Island, 1888
Photographer unknown

Evicted, New Bedford, Massachusetts, c. 1900
Photographer unknown

New Bedford, Massachusetts, c. 1900
Photographer unknown

Dump pickers, Providence, Rhode Island, 1903
Photographer unknown

Providence, Rhode Island, 1902
T. S. Bronson

Boston, Massachusetts, c. 1890
Photographer unknown

Kindergarten class, Manchester, New Hampshire, c. 1910   Photographer unknown

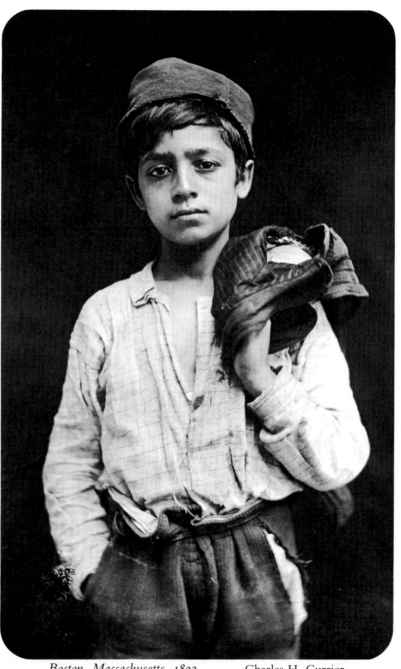

Youth

Boston, Massachusetts, 1892   Charles H. Currier

Boys are wild animals, rich in the treasures of sense, but the New England boy had a wider range of emotions than boys of more equable climates. . . . summer was drunken. Among senses, smell was the strongest — smell of hot pine-woods and sweet-fern in the scorching summer noons; of new-mown hay; of ploughed earth; of box hedges; of peaches, lilacs, syringas; of stables, barns, cow-yards; of salt water and low tide on the marshes. . . . Whether the children rolled in the grass, or waded in the brook, or swam in the salt ocean, or sailed in the bay, or fished for smelts in the creeks, or netted minnows in the salt-marshes, or took to the pine-woods and the granite quarries, or chased muskrats and hunted snapping-turtles in the swamps, or mushrooms or nuts on the autumn hills, summer and country were always sensual living . . .

—HENRY ADAMS
The Education of Henry Adams

Laconia, New Hampshire, c. 1900
Photographer unknown

It has been suggested that the Victorians "invented" childhood. Like all such generalizations, the truth of this assertion may be endlessly debated. Less open to debate is the early Puritans' belief in Predestination and Innate Depravity — harsh doctrines that made scant distinction between male or female, infant or adult. In the seventeenth and eighteenth centuries, a newborn child was assumed by the Puritans to be damned, until proven otherwise. Only in the nineteenth century did the sentimental notion of childhood innocence become widespread.

Some of the most charming nineteenth-century photographs in *This Was New England* are of children (pages 126, 132, and 133). On the other hand, some of the most heart-rending images also have children as their subjects (pages 127 and 150). The contrast was not lost on those early reformers who sought relief for the youthful victims of poverty, disease, and neglect.

Differences in social and economic status are also revealed in the series of schoolroom photographs in this section, which range from one of the earliest such photographs ever taken (page 143), to country schools (page 140), to city schools (page 141), to private academies (page 144), and colleges.

The images on pages 136 and 137, which recently came to light in the Manchester Historical Society, are special favorites of mine: here is public education that the fondest parents might wish for their children (or have wished for themselves).

The photograph on page 146 of an early medical class at the University of Vermont does not belong, strictly speaking, among these images. Yes, that *is* a cadaver. And when a medical student is thus confronted with mortality, his youth is at an end.

Manchester, New Hampshire, c. 1895   Ulric Bourgeois

Manchester, New Hampshire, c. 1895   Ulric Bourgeois

Berlin, Connecticut, 1864   Photographer unknown

Manchester, New Hampshire, c. 1900   Ulric Bourgeois

Ansonia, Connecticut, 1904
T. S. Bronson

Maple sugaring, Dover, Vermont, c. 1900
Porter Thayer

New Hampshire, c. 1885
John S. Wright

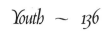

Kindergarten class, Manchester, New Hampshire, c. 1910
Photographer unknown

Kindergarten class, Manchester, New Hampshire, c. 1910
Photographer unknown

Kindergarten class, Manchester, New Hampshire, c. 1910

Photographer unknown

OVERLEAF: *Boston, Massachusetts, c. 1900* [Photographer unknown]

Brookline, Vermont, 1910

Porter Thayer

Fairhaven, Massachusetts, c. 1900   Photographer unknown

Vermont, c. 1885
Photographer unknown

Springfield, Massachusetts, c. 1895
Howes Brothers

Cape Cod, Massachusetts, c. 1860   Photographer unknown

Milton Academy, Milton, Massachusetts, c. 1900   Charles H. Currier

Reform school, Burlington, Vermont, c. 1880

Photographer unknown

Tufts Dental Infirmary, Boston, Massachusetts, 1909
Baldwin Coolidge

Vermont Medical School, Burlington, Vermont, c. 1880
Photographer unknown

Harvard Medical School, Boston, Massachusetts, 1893

Baldwin Coolidge

Nayatt Point,
Rhode Island, c. 1895
Photographer unknown

Gathering nuts, Kittery, Maine, 1892

Charles H. Currier

OVERLEAF: LEFT, *Factory, Woonsocket, Rhode Island, 1900;* RIGHT, *Newsboys, Providence, Rhode Island, 1903* [Photographers unknown]

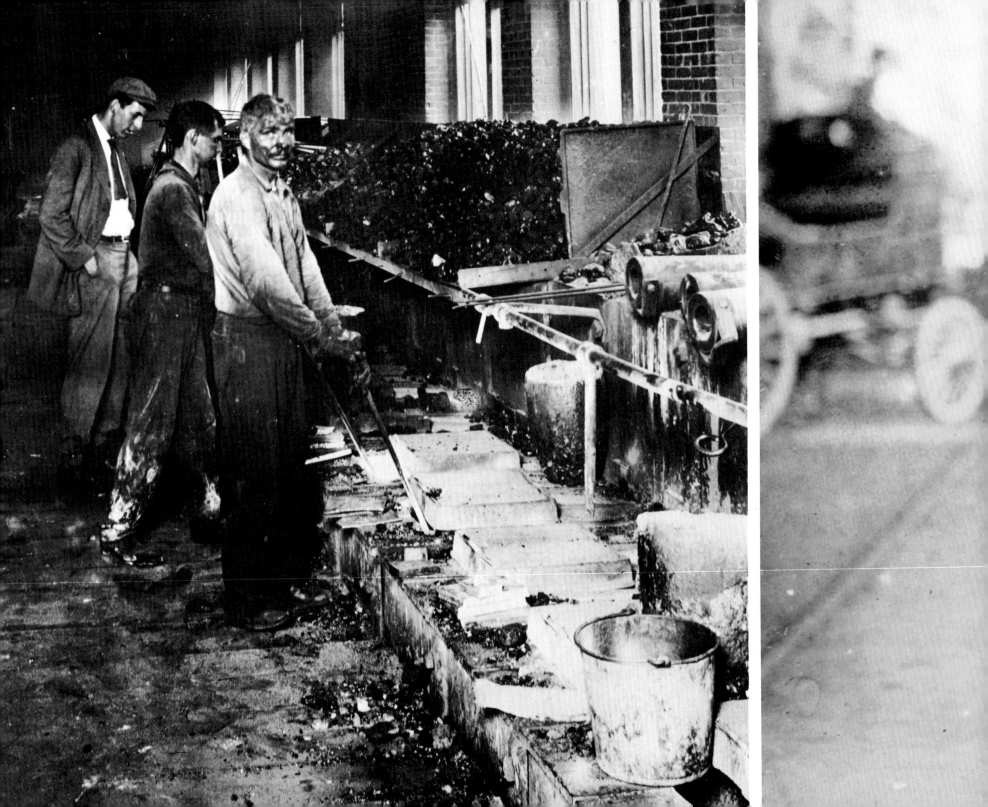

Silk-warping plant, Providence, Rhode Island, 1910   Photographer unknown

Work

At the loom, Newfane, Vermont, 1910   Porter Thayer

. . . *All other trades have here fallen into their ranks and places, to their great advantage; especially coopers and shoemakers, enriching themselves by their trades very much. Carpenters, joiners, glaziers, painters follow their trades only. Gunsmiths, locksmiths, blacksmiths, nailers, cutlers have left the plow. Weavers, brewers, bakers, costermongers, feltmakers, braziers, pewterers, and tinkers, rope-makers, masons, lime, brick and tile-makers, card-makers — to work and not to play. Turners, pumpmakers and wheelers, glovers, fellmongers and furriers, are orderly turned to their trades, besides divers sorts of shopkeepers, and some who have a mystery beyond others . . .*

—CAPTAIN EDWARD JOHNSON
Wonder-Working Providence of Sion's Saviour, *1654*

ABOVE: *Blacksmith shop, Dover, Vermont, 1902*
    Porter Thayer

Milford, Connecticut, 1908
W. H. Horton

The great German sociologist Max Weber was born in 1864 and died in 1920. His life thus spanned the period during which most of these photographs were taken — the period when the Industrial Revolution had been achieved, when all the extremes of wealth and misery that Karl Marx sought to redress were firmly in place. Perhaps Weber's most important contribution to our national self-understanding was a study, first published in English in 1930, titled *Protestant Ethic and the Spirit of Capitalism*. As generations of college students can attest, the book is heavy going. Yet it offers convincing solutions to a paradox that goes to the very heart of the New England experience.

Simply stated, the "Protestant Ethic" is the secular and material expression of a fundamental tenet of Puritanism (or, if you prefer, Calvinism): that the Devil finds work for idle hands, that only through unremitting labor may one be spared Hell's fire, and that the accumulation of capital (not the joyful spending of it) is a sign of salvation. The logic of Puritanism was doubtless lost on the thousands upon thousands of immigrants to New England whose religious beliefs differed from those of their Yankee masters. And by the 1850s, Yankee Puritans themselves had lost much of their original religious fervor. Their belief in hard work, however, and in the sanctity of capital, continued to shape New England society, as it does, to a degree, even now.

I have not chosen the photographs that follow to make a particular point, but rather to suggest the vast range of enterprises by which Yankees — native as well as foreign born, male and female, old and, alas, very young — struggled to earn a living. They document the life of workers in mills and factories (pages 164 and 165) and the persistence of cottage industries, tradesmen, and independent artisans (pages 153, 171 to 173). Among my own favorites are the sequence of logging images taken by Porter Thayer in

Newfane, Vermont, c. 1905

Porter Thayer

Vermont (pages 156 and 157) and of quarrymen at work (pages 159 to 161). (Most of these were taken by the Howes brothers.)

Again and again I am struck by the art and care photographers took capturing scenes of the hardest labor (page 154, top). Perhaps the most suggestive of all the photographs in this section is that of a group of Vermont copper miners (page 158). The man with the lantern is the mine owner himself. A religious man? How can one tell? But as the epitome of the "Protestant Ethic," he seems to stand for a whole class of men who sought salvation through thrift and self-denial and unremitting labor not so many years ago.

Newfane, Vermont, c. 1905
Porter Thayer

Copper miners, Royalton, Vermont, c. 1870   Photographer unknown

Quarry workers, Westfield, Massachusetts, c. 1895
Howes Brothers

Quarry workers, Westfield, Massachusetts, c. 1895

Howes Brothers

Quarry workers,
Barre, Vermont, 1894
Photographer unknown

Machine shop, Florence, Massachusetts, c. 1880
Photographer unknown

Machine shop interior, Waltham, Massachusetts, 1889
E. L. Sanderson

Cotton mill,
Adams, Massachusetts, 1880
Photographer unknown

Boston, Massachusetts, 1895

Charles H. Currier

Policeman, Springfield, Massachusetts, c. 1895
Howes Brothers

Boston, Massachusetts, c. 1890   Photographer unknown

New Britain, Connecticut, 1895
Howes Brothers

LEFT: *Montpelier, Vermont, c. 1890*
Photographer unknown

Messenger boys, Boston, Massachusetts, 1896
Photographer unknown

Preparing for ice harvest, Jamaica Plain, Massachusetts, 1895

Charles H. Currier

BELOW:

LEFT,
*Pawtucket,
Rhode Island, 1891*
Photographer unknown

RIGHT,
*Springfield,
Massachusetts, c. 1900*
Howes Brothers

Williamsville, Vermont, 1910
Porter Thayer

Western Massachusetts, c. 1890
Howes Brothers

LEFT: *Northampton, Massachusetts, 1885*
Howes Brothers

Western Massachusetts, c. 1885
Howes Brothers

Tree sprayers, Windsor Locks, Connecticut, 1885
Howes Brothers

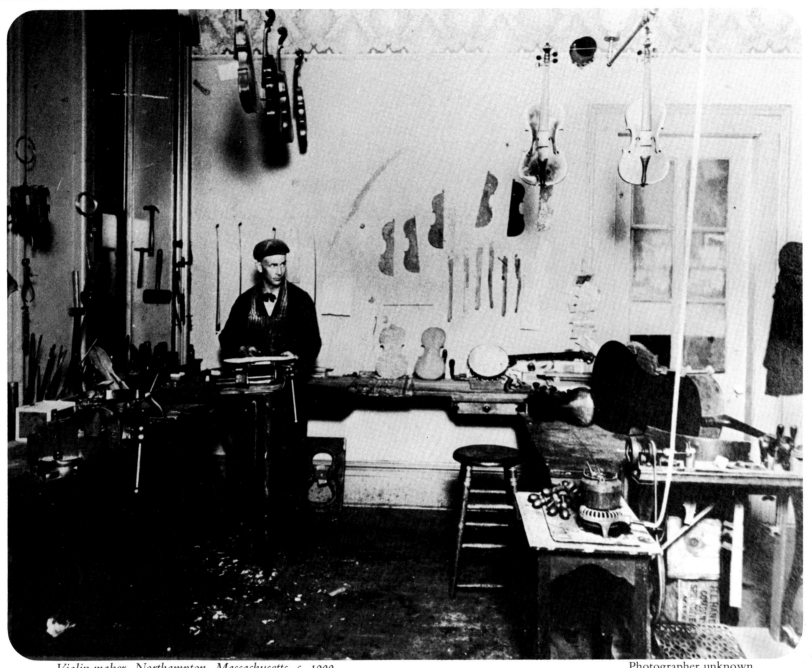

Violin maker, Northampton, Massachusetts, c. 1900

Photographer unknown

Barbershop, Concord, New Hampshire, c. 1890
Photographer unknown

Photographer's studio, New Haven, Connecticut, 1867
Myron T. Filley

Western Massachusetts, c. 1905
Howes Brothers

General store, West Dover, Vermont, 1909
Porter Thayer

Drugstore, Springfield, Massachusetts, 1891

Howes Brothers

Business Exposition,
Concord, New Hampshire, c. 1885
Photographer unknown

Quincy Market, Boston, Massachusetts, 1895
Photographer unknown

Sayles Finishing Plant, Saylesville, Rhode Island, c. 1920   Photographer unknown

A Company Town

Sayles company playground   Photographer unknown

I leap from the town into a large mill, with five hundred employees, and say to the master, "How about the dwellings of your operatives? How many hours do they have at home?" "Well, I hope they don't have any. The best-ventilated place they are ever in is my mill. They had better stay here sixteen hours out of the twenty-four; it keeps them out of mischief better than any other place. As long as they work, they are not doing worse." . . .

—WENDELL PHILLIPS
The Foundations of the Labor Movement

Company office, Saylesville, Rhode Island, c. 1920
Photographer unknown

Company drivers, Saylesville, Rhode Island, c. 1920
Photographer unknown

In the year 1817, two men named Patrick Jackson and Nathan Appleton constructed a series of factories along the Merrimac River in Massachusetts. In order to avoid using child labor (and immigrants, it seems) Jackson and Appleton decided to build a company town around these factories to which they could attract "respectable females" from the outlying farm communities. They named their community in memory of Francis Cabot Lowell, who had been their partner but who had died some three years earlier.

Lowell, Massachusetts, became New England's first company town. The workers were provided with company housing, company stores, company churches, and other recreational and educational facilities. However, the company soon passed into other hands and Lowell, like all other company towns we know of, became a crowded, unhealthy place where workers were exploited to the very limit.

At the turn of the century, another New England company town came into existence. This was Saylesville, Rhode Island, the home of the Sayles Finishing Corporation. As with the early Lowell operation, it seems that the original owners of the Saylesville factories intended to create a community with a decent company store, company post office, and company police and fire departments. There were company playgrounds for employees' children, daily recreational activities for workers, and regular company-wide picnics and outings.

The photographs in this section were all taken by company photographers for the official house organ. Perhaps they are misleading, but the people do not seem to be restive or downtrodden. What we do know for certain, however, is that within ten years from the time these photographs were taken, a series of labor strikes rocked the Sayles Finishing Corporation and the factories and company town closed their doors forever.

Company gate, Saylesville, Rhode Island, c. 1920   Photographer unknown

Company outing, Saylesville, Rhode Island, c. 1920

Photographer unknown

Foremen's outing, Saylesville, Rhode Island, c. 1920
Photographer unknown

All photographs on the facing page are of Saylesville,
    Rhode Island, c. 1920, photographers unknown.
    ABOVE: LEFT, *Yard crew*
        RIGHT, *Color shop, Plant C*
    BELOW: LEFT, *Company fire department*
        RIGHT, *Printing Room, Plant C*

Noonday Baseball League, Saylesville, Rhode Island, c. 1920
Photographer unknown

Company outing, Saylesville, Rhode Island, c. 1920　　　　　Photographer unknown

Employees on outing, Saylesville, Rhode Island, c. 1920   Photographer unknown

World's Greatest Sleigh Party, Concord, New Hampshire, c. 1900   Photographer unknown

The Day Off

New Hampshire coast, c. 1890   Photographer unknown

Perhaps what most moves us in winter is some reminiscence of far-off summer. . . . The cold is merely superficial; it is summer still at the core, far, far, within.

—HENRY DAVID THOREAU
Journal, *VII*, *112*, *January 11, 1855*

New Hampshire, c. 1890
Photographer unknown

BELOW: LEFT, *Curling, Boston Common, 1897* [Charles H. Currier]
RIGHT, *Vermont, c. 1900* [Photographer unknown]

As spring follows a long winter, so, in the nineteenth century, New England Puritans slowly threw off the grip of the Angry God of the Colonial era. On the Sabbath pious families still forbade play and spent many hours in church or meetinghouse. Dancing and theatergoing were still considered sinful by the more conservative Protestant sects. "Leisure time," as we think of it today, was in short supply even among the most affluent; and it was proportionately scarcer among working-class families.

But the thaw was well under way by mid-century. Newport and Nahant, which were among New England's first summer resorts, were soon joined by countless other summer colonies (few of such opulence, of course) both along the shore and inland. Excursion steamers crowded with "day-trippers" plied New England lakes and rivers, as well as coastal waters. Members of fish and game clubs, outing societies, and fraternal organizations made the best of even the briefest holidays. Yachting, tennis, cycling, skating, iceboating — whatever the season, whatever the occasion, "the day off" was cause for celebration.

And whatever the season, our early photographers were there to celebrate with the rest. Indeed, it was the great contrast in changing New England seasons that, as it does today, offered such diverse opportunities for recreation as the winter scene on page 197 and the summer scene on page 204. As was the case throughout this period, photographers who focused their cameras on those enjoying their day off were able to capture a way of life (page 206) that in less than seventy-five years has all but entirely vanished.

Iceboats, Maine, c. 1900

N. L. Stebbins

New Haven, Connecticut, 1907   T. S. Bronson

Cape Cod, Massachusetts, 1900

Frederic Perry

Fishing stand, Cuttyhunk, Massachusetts, c. 1880

Albert Cook Church

New Hampshire coast, c. 1890
Photographer unknown

New Hampshire coast, c. 1890
Photographer unknown

Maine, 1894
Charles H. Currier

Maine, c. 1885
John S. Wright

Harris Falls, Connecticut, c. 1900
Photographer unknown

Milton, Massachusetts, c. 1910

T. S. Bronson

Lake Massapesic, New Hampshire, c. 1900

Ulric Bourgeois

South Boston, Massachusetts, 1898

Henry Peabody

Lake Quanapaug, Connecticut, 1906   T. S. Bronson

Newport, Rhode Island, c. 1895   Photographer unknown

Lighthouse Point, New Haven, Connecticut, c. 1915   T. S. Bronson

OVERLEAF: *Haven family, Boston, Massachusetts, 1868*   [James W. Black]

New Bedford, Massachusetts, c. 1865
Photographer unknown

Newport, Rhode Island, c. 1890   Photographer unknown

Clambake, Barnstable, Massachusetts, c. 1900

Edward Sprague

New Bedford, Massachusetts, c. 1900

Albert Cook Church

Country fair, Barnstable, Massachusetts, c. 1900

Edward Sprague

Cricket team, Boston, Massachusetts, 1896
Charles H. Currier

Providence, Rhode Island, c. 1880
Photographer unknown

Waltham, Massachusetts, 1889
E. L. Sanderson

Newtown, Connecticut, 1908

T. S. Bronson

Acknowledgments

Mrs. Laura Abbot, Vermont Historical Society
Mrs. Kay Bader, Snow Library, Orleans, Massachusetts
Mr. Leroy Bellamy, Prints and Photographs Division, Library of Congress
Mr. William Bunting, Portland, Maine
Mr. William Cholmers, Freeport, Maine
Mr. David Corrigan, New Haven Colony Historical Society
Mr. William Crosley, New Hampshire Historical Society
Mr. Sam Daniel, Prints and Photographs Division, Library of Congress
Mr. Rob Egleston, New Haven Colony Historical Society
Mr. Richard Franz, New Hampshire Historical Society
Mr. Alan Greenberg, Forbes Library, Northampton, Massachusetts
Mrs. Shirley Greene, Washington, D.C.
Mr. Douglas Hallett, Falmouth (Mass.) Historical Society
Mrs. Bernice Hammond, Newport, Rhode Island
Mrs. Norma Harris, Ashfield (Mass.) Historical Society
Mr. Theodore Hendrick, Southampton, Massachusetts
Mrs. Holly Hopewell-Bowman, Forbes Library, Northampton, Massachusetts
Mr. Walter Hurlburt, Kennebunkport, Maine
Mr. Gerald Kearns, Prints and Photographs Division, Library of Congress
Mrs. Joan Paterson Kerr, New Haven, Connecicut
Mrs. Edith LaFrancis, Agawam, Massachusetts
Mrs. Elizabeth Lasard, Manchester (N.H.) Historical Association
Mr. Burton Lavallee, Cranston, Rhode Island
Mr. Daniel Lohnes, Society for the Preservation of New England Antiquities, Boston, Massachusetts
Mr. Robert Lovell, Sandwich (Mass.) Historical Society
Mr. Richard McKenney, Cape Cod Community College
Mrs. Alice Manning, Northampton, Massachusetts
Ms. Phyllis Manning, Saco, Maine
Ms. Martha Mayo, Locks and Canals Collection, Lowell, Massachusetts
Mrs. Timothy Meekers, Stowe, Vermont
Mrs. Jean Nugent, Lee, New Hampshire
Mrs. Marjorie Owen, Old Colony Historical Society, Taunton, Massachusetts
Mrs. Frederic Perry, Barnstable, Massachusetts
Ms. Marsha Peters, Rhode Island Historical Society
Mrs. Virginia Pliesto, Manchester (N.H.) Historical Association
Mr. Phillip Purrington, New Bedford Whaling Museum
Mr. Francis S. Smith, Portland, Maine
Mr. Joseph Johnson Smith, New Haven Colony Historical Society
Mrs. Mary Sprague, Barnstable, Massachusetts
Mr. Charles Spencer, Rutland, Vermont
Mr. Charles Spooner, Falmouth, Massachusetts
Mrs. Porter Thayer, Williamsville, Vermont
Mrs. Alice Towle, Kingston, Rhode Island
Mrs. Annabelle Trayser, Trayser Memorial Museum, Barnstable, Massachusetts
Mr. John Wilmerding, Dartmouth College
Mr. Walter M. Wright, Baker Library, Dartmouth College

This Was New England is, in the happiest sense, a collaborative venture. My debt to those who have so patiently advised and guided me is past counting. I fear it is inevitable that by inadvertence I have omitted from this list the names of certain individuals whose contributions are very real. I can only hope that they will find the book itself some reward for their kindness.

New Hampshire coast, c. 1890
Photographer unknown

Sources

All photographs not listed below are from
the Sandler Collection.

Courtesy of the Ashfield (Mass.) Historical Society:
page 173 *top*

Courtesy of Cape Cod Community College: page 97

Courtesy of the Dartmouth College Library: pages
28–29

Courtesy of the Forbes Library, Northampton, Massachusetts: pages 118, 120, 162 *top*, 175

Collection of Mrs. Edith LaFrancis: pages 65 *bottom*, 68
bottom, 72, 73, 74, 75, 78, 82, 89, 159, 160, 166, 169 *top*, 171
bottom right, 172, 173 *bottom*, 177 *top*, 178

Courtesy of the Library of Congress: pages 21, 34, 40
bottom, 42, 43, 44 *top*, 45, 50, 52 *bottom*, 58–59, 64, 85 *bottom*,
87, 88, 93, 94 *top*, 98, 111, 113, 115, 117, 127, 144, 149, 150
left, 161, 163, 164, 165, 170, 192, 194 *bottom left*, 202 *top*,
206, 213, 217 *top*

Courtesy of the Manchester (N.H.) Historical Association: pages 126, 136, 137

Courtesy of the New Bedford Whaling Museum: pages
23, 27, 39, 40 *top*, 46, 47, 53, 62 *top*, 79, 95, 99, 105, 112,
122, 135, 141, 202 *bottom*, 215

Courtesy of the New Hampshire Historical Society:
pages 20, 25 *bottom*, 96 *bottom*, 176 *top*, 179

Courtesy of the New Haven Colony Historical Society: pages 16, 22, 33, 36–37, 70–71, 96 *top*, 114, 134 *top*, 176
bottom, 197, 209, 220

Courtesy of the Rhode Island Historical Society: pages
25 *top*, 92, 110, 116, 121 *bottom*, 123 *top*, 148, 150–151, 152,
171 *bottom left*, 182, 183, 184, 186, 187, 188, 189, 190, 191,
217 *bottom*

Courtesy of the Snow Library, Orleans, Massachusetts: pages 56, 84 *left*

Courtesy of the Society for the Preservation of New
England Antiquities: pages 28 *left*, 38, 48 *left*, 48–49, 57, 60,
80, 81, 86 *bottom*, 90, 91 *top*, 104, 106 *bottom*, 108, 109, 119,
121 *top*, 124–125, 138–139, 146 *top*, 147, 167, 169 *bottom*,
180–181, 196, 210–211, 212

Courtesy of Mrs. Porter Thayer: pages 17, 24, 66, 67,
68 *top*, 85 *top*, 86 *top*, 91 *bottom*, 134 *bottom*, 140, 153, 154 *top*,
156, 157, 171 *top*, 177 *bottom*

Courtesy of Mrs. Annabelle Trayser, Trayser Memorial Museum: pages 52 *top*, 54, 94 *bottom*, 143, 198, 214, 216

Courtesy of the Vermont Historical Society: pages 35,
69, 76, 142 *top*, 145, 146 *bottom*, 158, 168, 194 *bottom right*

Courtesy of the Waltham (Mass.) Historical Society:
pages 162 *bottom*, 218–219

The photograph on this page was a particular favorite of Mitchell Ford. To those of us who knew him, it is not a surprising selection, for it is a gentle picture with a genuine sense of humor. Mitchell Ford was a gentle man, a creative genius whose sense of humor touched all with whom he came into contact. We shall not forget him.

Designed by Mitchell Ford.
Calligraphy by Samuel Bryant.
Composed in Bembo and Blado
    by DEKR Corporation, of Woburn, Massachusetts.
Printed in two impressions
    by Eastern Press, New Haven,
    on Mountie Velvet Dull,
    stock made by Northwest Paper Corporation
    and supplied by Paper Sales Corporation.
Bound in G.S.B. Fabrics Corporation's book cloth
    by A. Horowitz and Son, Fairfield, New Jersey.